for when you decide to be honest

Barbara "Simi" Muhumuza

Barbara "Simi" Muhumuza

ISBN: 1720694818
ISBN-13: 978-1720694816

for when you decide to be honest

CONTENTS

for when you decide to be honest

for yourself

the most important vow

patience

speak responsibly

how to care for an orlenadar

worry not

stardust

remain

don't let it win today

no.

seen

thank you

on who I am

when the black girl goes missing

attached to this promise

not a poem but a promise

no superman needed

talk to your mothers' mother

both

hey you

listen to a black woman today

a daughter's brew

little mermaid

the lying child

before the dark girl knew love

prison transfer

Barbara "Simi" Muhumuza

father's daughter

inside him

when the goodbye has meaning

thank God

when I was 9

existing to be forgotten

issa insecurity

we must no longer

acknowledgments

for when you decide to be honest

"perfection will always be fleeting, love yourself deep in the mess of everything else"

above all, I hope reading this brings you to a place of understanding

for when you decide to be honest

the honesty

are there lions walking around there?

it is the beginning of 9th grade
and I am a belly full of violent butterflies
reminding me that fear exists
even during daytime

I tell my mom,
"drop me off on the corner"

so that eyes do not see
how Africa has made a home
out of her face, I forget
myself as a carbon copy
mirrored, even if only in pieces

I've spent my adolescence preparing
nights spent scrubbing heritage
out of my skin
peeling off my (de)scent

I must shape shift
into the kind of black
they won't shy away from

I am covered
in the haze of worry
when I find my seat
in my first class

eyes now glued to my body
the weight of their wonder
heavy on my bones

I have filled my mouth
with the answers to their curiosity

I tell them
"yes, lions do exist there"

for when you decide to be honest

but it is here
where we are prey,
the way we slip through
the jaws of this land
entering the throat
with flags still hanging
off our necks
coming out the end
everything but recognizable

tips for job hunting while black (I)

scrub your mouth with affirmative action
cut out your voice
glue the sound back into a song for beggars
burn down the hair that reaches for the sun
do not reach for the sun
find a tree
unfold it like an umbrella atop your head
shade the corners of your pride white
become familiar with the dance of disappearance

be reminded that you are only here
to be the centerpiece for their diversity
your body is not useful if not caged,
or glimmering in a glass box
say nothing of your descent
nothing of how you are a mighty meteor
originated from constellations of women
who showed you how to fly
do not show them that you can fly
they will pluck the galaxy from your wings
until the stars are nostalgia smoldering in your iris

tips for job hunting while black (II)

change the colors of your eyes
maybe, a brown with a flicker of gold
remind them of the boundless value
attached to your being
become an open land prepared for colonization
when they come, you mustn't let
your blood thrash into a riot with the sand
bend your body down into a prayer,
the weight of the Bible will keep you grounded anyway

they will ask you why you are the best fit for their company
"how can you transform us into the subtle lingerer of slavery?"
say that you are affirmative sound
a song that's begging to reach for the sun
unfolding like a dance of disappearance
originating from women that show you how to be
boundless treasure tied to land prepared for reaping

when the colonizers come

they will see your body
and imagine it a casket
a burial haven for their guilt

they will deceive you
into thinking you are famished
that your belly is not a full house
of pride and laughter

they will talk about the ways
they can rebuild your home
as if they are not the reason
it is still choking to death
on the dust its' own ash

america to the people

can you tell me who you'd be
without the imprint
of all that has been
smeared on your legacy?

would you know how to love
if your heart did not know
the grief of loss?

did you forget that
in this place,
pain is mandatory
for your existence?

do you not remember
that spines must split
for you to have this
allegiance?

not survival

don't exist
too loudly now
too much black
in this white space
is how graveyards
fill to the brim
with bodies
that only knew
how to be human

every ounce of humanity

there was always humanity
for all to see
within the way you blinked
to keep dirt out of the eye

within the way
sweat sat neatly
atop your brow

within the way
your body had no choice
but to protect you

and I wonder
if they could not see
or refused to notice
your humanity
when your body was
behind the barrels
of their guns

an american stench

you can smell death here
the scent thick on the necks
of black bodies
draping the limbs
like a loud cologne

they don't know
the way our mothers pray, beg
we won't be black corpses
turned criminal, embalmed
 into a memory today

do they know how
mothers twine heaven into our skin
in hopes that they will see God
should they decide to unravel us?

sticky nights

my skin is facing extinction
and I can't stop dreaming
of fire filled nights
sticky with the stench of freedom

⅗ of space

we are undressing
stripping pride from
stomach linings

pleading, welts of strife
on the foundation of bodies

rage charring the skull
yet still convincing ourselves
that God does not scorch cities
for salvation

frantically searching
for the clothing of humanity

hoping to lose the shadow of ⅗
hoping to be whole underneath the sun too

digesting silver bullets
and still not bleeding as a human

we are wondering how to be human

should we pull the skeleton
from this house of skin?

should we (b)r(e)athe white
like the marrow of bone?

should we pretend
forge a story of progress
act like we are not
suffocating beneath the soil?

an August 9th anniversary

Today is one of those hard days where the lingering pain and rage swallow
all the bone.
Today is the day we remember one of the souls that ignited the fire of this
forever burning flame.
Today is the day we remember Mike Brown and all he was before he
became a Martyr for the sake of this war we've been fighting.
I remember him and try to imagine all the ways he was human
before he was a hashtag,
before he became the face of a movement he didn't ask to be a part of,
before he got killed for being **black**, and **alive**.

I imagine him dreaming and imagining his future and become saddened at
how quickly it all was taken away from him.
I imagine the void his family must endure.
I imagine what he would feel now knowing that his name is being said and
that he is recognized. Mike Brown was one of many.
I just hope he's somewhere where he can be black and human, and without
fear that he'll be killed for being only what he knows how.
To this day, we're still burning cities for you and all the others.
We continue to keep rage in the pockets of our hearts for you.

charred fingertips

how much higher
must I stretch my hands
for you to see me?

the sun chars the ends of my fingers
sweat has swallowed all my innocence
and is falling off my edges

what more should I do to show you
I'm burning with the want to stay alive?

in remembrance

knotted in the gut of soil
you'll find the dialect of past
men, women, children
osseous matter, a maggots' feast

we awaken with nightmares
still attached to the sweat of night
hanging from clenched jaws
drums of home, echoing

rather omit, than speak
the ache of remembrance
rather purge, than digest
this prying grief

the definition of Black

I don't mean when served without milk,
as in, a cafe noir. Nor reflecting little
Light or the heavy weight of evening.
And I don't mean connected

With especially the devil
Or relating to covert intelligence operations
from the enemy country. Nor the promise
of a disaster, the vengeance of our mother

just begging to be unleashed. What I mean
is singing with my tribe,
at the church built from carnage --
for our souls to unclench. Our mouths

the opposite of white, a pigmentation of joy.
What I mean is, an army of survival,
a parade of jazz, an ebony of brilliance. What I mean,
is everything but what they wrote us out to be.

this and only this

and it is only with perseverance,
that we find ourselves
and our honest survival
under the rubble of great strife

breathe

you magnetic force
it's okay,

breathe.

you've risen from the ash
there's still so much left to do
but for now,

breathe.

let this moment bind itself
around your heart
you're still here,

breathe.

grandmother's dream

the tale of you and I

where love
becomes a monument
of truth

this is where fate is birthed
where destiny is bred

where you and I begin

in the cushions
of grandmother's dream
between the synapses
of her delight

winter resurrection

the earth loses nothing
in winter
all the green plucked
from the root

but what remains
blooms bigger than soil
could ever conceive

and it is this alchemy
that reminds me
to inhale
during the cold season

it is this cycle
that births the understanding
that this undoing
is vital
to my becoming

two blazing hearts

on Sunday morning
we fold ourselves in sin
between the pressure of
radiant desire

convince ourselves that God
will forgive us

for this is a love that can
and will always
illuminate dim cities

and God wants nothing
but to see the combustion
of us in between
a twilight heaven

say it loudly

why do you shy away
when you speak
about the price
of your love?

you should be
body upright
tongue ignited
fists steady
screaming to the world
what you warrant

for when you decide to be honest

dream invasion

I dream of loving you
in front of the sun,
under the whisper of God
with the blessing of ancestors

stages of our song

the breath in the rise and fall waltz
you perform in the morning
with your skin elongated across your chest
before the birds accompany
before the sun fractures the sky open

the shifting of skin
against sheets
against bones
the way our frames envelope into each other
ready to compose a great score

these are the stages of our song
the hymn of unraveling
a tune sewn softly into throat tissue
patiently waiting to play the first note
for the world to hear

not a poem but a call to action

when he proves that he is incapable of loving you
do not fantasize about his possible capabilities
to uphold the attachment

he displayed his piercing truth
denying it doesn't further the distance
between yourself and loneliness

it only brings you closer to it

when it comes time to make that choice
look in the mirror and choose
only what glares right back

for yourself

the aftermath of forgiveness looks like
fire that decides to be merciful
that decides to stop incinerating what
could've been from the inside out

that no longer salivates at the biting
scent of revenge,
that prays for something altered
like a flowering bound of restoration
like a life without this gnawing ache

like an understanding
that this was crucial
for this rise
this renewal

the most important vow

vow to show up for yourself
just as the seasons
on time, and with purpose

patience

just wait
until the guidance
of spirits
feel them remind you
of Love
without despair

speak responsibly

be mindful of the weight of words
of the heaviness of language
of the responsibility of speaking

how to care for an Oleander

be careful of where you plant her
you should know that she buds

best in full sun, she is brave enough for shade
but only in doses, as big as pins and needles

she will slip you into a new sleeve
build a new color of your eyes

and if you love her, there is
no going back, as in

you must give all of you to her
crawl on all your good bones

let the smoke of her poison
devour all of who you were before her

she will be nothing like a weed
creeping through the concrete

but everything similar to a bed of roses
enticing, donning thorns and drawing blood,

when plucked from her soil
when she is in full bloom

she exists all over the place,
and holds death at the bridge,

of her mouth, if you inhale her
expect your heart to burst

into a disarray, she will leave
her scent in your throat

a reminder of the resurrection
that awaits, should she ever

bloom for you again

worry not

the truest, boldest,
most fearless love
is freedom

always freedom

if you love them
you will let them fly

worry not about the sky
they choose to soar

stardust

each star dipped in
your pool of skin
before being neatly placed
in the night sky

galaxies birthed in each
space you breathe
in each body you love

the moon is envious
of the way you shine

remain

remain where you are revered
celebrated for every fragment
of who you are
loved, even on the days
when limbs feel downcast

darling, stay with those
that still recognize
the sunshine in you
on your lightless days

don't let it win today

when you can feel the shifting of the earth
and hear your name in the sludge of soil
and see your face cracking in between
the clouds of a salmon sky

remember that it is all in rotation for you

know that you can win this war of sorrow
this battle that rips bliss from the origin
know that you can make it to
to the edge of survival

understand that your body
is not ready to bow down
to gravity

not yet

no.

for many moons
frames may have slipped
shattered in between
the homes of mouths

but when I say no
the meaning does not
suspend itself

in this splitting moment
no revokes what was
congests the air of what is

and every fiber of you
should not refuse me

this choice

seen

I see you, black girl
you'll never be invisible to me
I'll burn cities down in your name

thank you

to all the woman before me
I came in pieces
in confusing bits
unaware of the world
and yet,
you allowed a space for me
thank you

on who I am

the black girl that's trying to put herself together through her writing.
the black girl that's trying to be black and girl without burning.
the black girl that's trying to be black and in love without resistance.
the black girl that's trying to not let her name get lost in the grime of everything else.
the black girl that has the names of other black girls attached to every part of her.
the black girl that loves the black men that recognize her full humanity.
the black girl that really doesn't give a fuck about your opinion.
the black girl that will protect other black girls until the end of everything.
the black girl that burns in rage, all the time.
the glowing black girl.
the angry black girl.
the missing black girl.
the invisible black girl.
all titles they'd rather call me than my name.
the black girl, here, existing.

when the black girl goes missing

no, there is not a shotgun scream of worry
stretching through the horizon

no, there is not an interrupted nightfall
footprints of animals tracking the scent of death

no, there are not screens of beaming faces
reminding all the hijacked joy

there are no hashtag names
flashing through a digital town

there are no half-hung men
tangled in the rope of the righteous

there is no chant of sorrow
scattering across the sea

there are piles of shattered bones
stacked puzzles, pulsating in plain site

there is waist deep silence
skin roasting beneath the eager sun

there are forgotten coils of wool hair
broken fingers reaching for the sky

there are cries to God,
there are crying gods

there are black girls
some 60,000

missing, lost
melting through the cracks

existing knowing that
they will be forgotten

like a distant whisper,
battling with the wind

for when you decide to be honest

an empty grave
bare tombstone

attached to this promise

The world won't protect black girls
but I promise,
I'll **burn it all** down in their names.

not a poem but a promise

From disappearance to death, the existence of black girls and women is often ignored. Every day, I try to figure out how I can do more. I think of how I should be doing more because there's so much to be done. I think of how the world won't do anything despite there being so much to be done. It's irritating and frustrating realizing that all that should be done, could be done if someone just spent a moment actually listening to a black woman, or a black girl in need. This is not about reprimanding black girls for not protecting themselves, this is about the lack of communal effort to protect them. This is about the lack of urgent need to talk to our black boys/men and teach them to not be predatory. This is about learning and understanding that there's nothing that can be done ALONE to prevent sexual assault, and abuse, and death against black girls and women.

This is about understanding that what needs to be done is up to all of us. This is about reversing the effects of rape culture. This is about protecting our girls and not only just that but respecting their personal agency. I want to be deeply involved in the development of young black girls, and not to teach them what not to be but to teach them and help them understand that they can be anything and that they should be everything they desire because they deserve to exist without reprimand. I want to help them feel protected and heard and seen -- things that I never truly experienced until recently. I want to help them see that their lives should be more than just their survival but their success. I want to protect them and love them and help them move mountains. And you should too. Black girls matter. Black women matter. Not because of all they do, but simple because they are.

no superman needed

God's greatest gift
this ancestral continuation
this black wizardry

these limbs
branched in tune
with the influence
of before

yet, still,
cultivating an energy
of my own

everyday,
becoming superwoman
and saving my own world

talk to your mother's mother

when the fragments of womanhood
meddle between your bones
coat you in the dust
of your mother's mother

guard your core
like the brawn
of second flesh

call unto your ancestors

that tribe of women
that weaved your worth
into your mouth
braided your throat
into a hum of survival

call unto them, when pride
has made a swollen disarray
of the man

call unto them, when he begins
to hemorrhage into forces
that do not believe
in the existence of your choice

both

being black is knowing
that your bleached skeleton
is your only evidence of humanity

being woman is knowing
a fissured pelvis
is still not enough blood
for the world to believe in wolves

being both is knowing
a cursed culture
that unravels ancient wounds

being both is knowing
that oppression has been
branded into tarred pink filled tissue

to never be recognized
until you are the half of
a divided hell

until you are
fragmented column
of the American scripture

until you are draining into
shattered mirrors
wondering which crucial
creation to abandon

hey you

with the trombone hips
the walk of jazz and midnight

with the shattered shards for teeth
blood hanging on every word

with hands that trail the silhouette
of every shadowed corner

with the love laced smile

with the name buried underneath
patched inside forgotten tissue

with African threaded pores
war the flavor of your nightmares

do you know that I see you?

do you know that I love you anyway?

did you listen to a black woman today?

reach inside a black woman's throat
you'll find galaxies
lamenting howls transformed
into supernova shacks of life
of love
of everything you should dare
not ignore

a daughters brew

i would have named you
after the broken-chords
of my grandmother's song

nnkunda

she would sing
when she knew
my mother was still
too much girl
for all the womanhood
the world would siphon from her

come home

daughter

come home

you are
not done brewing
in my belly
she would sing

little mermaid

when my brother was 5, he had a doll
her red hair would splash
underneath the bright sky
like the beginning of a rainbow
the abstruse model of his existence

our family imagined that, at 5
there was a bottomless oblivion
that he, would soon let the doll go
and curl underneath the weight
of machismo

but even at 5, he looked at me with eyes
that knew the business of identity

the way it haunts the
counterfeit
archetype
of your being

barely caressing your core
like a shadow underneath
the scope of the sun
waiting until the freedom of night
to become one with all of you

the lying child

when I was 12, I taught myself
how to lie, twisted my mouth
into loops, made wolves
with the hole of my mouth

I fed my chant slowly,
into the ears of those
dying of thirst
from my girlhood flame

it was the only way I knew how
to take my body back
remove this too soon bruise
from the pool of my navel

wolves could not exist
unless I made them
drew them up with my teeth

because then, I would not
smell their scent on my flesh
because then, I would not have
shame gnawing on my muscle

because then, if I just
give my throat to everything
I will not grow tired
of bellowing bloody truths

with no one willing to hear me

before the dark girl knew love

I tell my mom
I want to wear a brighter face to school
if I do, the boys will no longer
render me a filthy bruise

I denounce this strangle of flesh
constricting me into the hue of muck

I wish to be curls of silk
a freckled face that knows nothing of disgust
I dream of tubes of chemical warfare
imagine my skin cracking underneath a new dawn
a newly peppered bright girl

blossoming

prison transfer

before the bellow of the crow
and the slither of dew

before the creaking of restless bones
straightening for the demands of time

before hands that find warmth
pulsating next to theirs

before the mother caresses
the cheeks of her children

before the father stumbles
into a house he no longer belongs

before the lovers shred lust
between their jagged joints

sirens stretch through a splitting morning
enough to rend a swaying dream

the weighted shackles hang
between the eclipse of then and now

they will be jailed before
the world is awake to protest

camouflaged humanity
draped in a swarm of orange

during the hymn of transfer
I think of my father

I wonder if he is searching for life
in his reflection between steel doors

I pray he still remembers
what my face looks like

underneath a morning sun

father's daughter

you wear your mother's face in the shade,
fearful that the sun will pull your father
limb by limb, from each eye

the slow tap dance of lesions
drape your feet first
glide their way up
crowd the fuzz of your brows

unfold you with the shimmer of your reflection
his smile splits your face in half
your virtuous mother nowhere to be found

the flutter of two decades
and you still cannot escape him

like dead tissue
reluctant to decompose
he is still entangled in all of you

inside him

auntie, there is nothing left of you
you are the the hue of a black blue sky
all night I hear his ghosts, bouncing
off the floorboards

they have grown tired of your hosting

I see all of him erupt in the stir of your sleep
you have been mangled split and left to perish

why did you ever leave home?

you told me to make no room for silence

to fill the corners of every space
show them that womanhood is not
a withering flower, but a threatening
howl of existence

I look to you and do not see the woman of wild rain
of crowing, and unfolding mornings
of leaping, echoing pride

I do not see the woman with gun-powdered skin

but I see him, resting in your core
the color of a blood-filled dusk
reconstructing your bridged ribs
cementing out your hollow voice

I see you
pinned into a question mark
behind the cage of his steel-cloaked chest

you taught me to never build a home
made from the bones of men
but it is there, under a jagged shadow
that I see you

veiled and disappearing in your fear
of being lonely

when goodbye has meaning

I'm learning to look back
on my honesty
and not shy away
from the person I was then

not let knots of fear
pull me away
from the truth of before

there is beauty in this growth
in this knowing that the past
is now a distant
uncommon moment

something that enfolded me
into the current
but ultimately,
controls me no longer

thank God

crumble into a new bed of soil
grow into a new form of flower
bud a new scent of triumph
thank God for surviving
another dark season

for when you decide to be honest

the understanding

for when you decide to be honest

on what has helped shape my honesty

When I was 9: The Stolen Joy Of Black Girlhood

For most of my adolescence, I was considered an "overdeveloped" girl. As a young girl, with my father's height, and my mother's hips attached to my being, I was declined my right to conventional girlhood — to be a girl before the weight that comes with womanhood, and consensual sexual endeavors. Genuine girlhood, the kind that many black girls are denied, is the right to be a girl, without the unnecessary gender restrictions, that is free to experience the fullness of herself — explore her developing body, mind and spirit without the predatory intrusion of men (or women because sexual assault/harassment is not only from men), and with all the protection from family, friends, and the community. The aforementioned, however, is not something I can say I ever experienced, and I'm sure that many black women can attest to the same sentiment.

When I was 9, I received my first vaginal blood flow. My period had come to me while I was in class at my elementary school. Many of my peers and teachers weren't prepared for something like that at the time, so I was sent home. I was told not to be embarrassed even though there was blood all over my skirt, and legs. Along with being told not to be ashamed, I was also told to enjoy this introduction to "womanhood," and although I understood the gist of what that meant, I still felt very much like a girl. A girl that could bleed now, but still a girl. I wasn't ready for womanhood, and I didn't think that blood made me ready either. I learned quickly though that my opinion on womanhood didn't matter because under the gaze of the rest of the world, men mainly, I was now a woman. I was now a woman and considered a person to objectify at every given opportunity.

Shortly after Mother Nature made an appearance in my life, so did the rest of the misinterpreted "gifts" that come with her like the more developed body, and the attention of boys. I had always dealt with boys as a girl, but always in the traditional, very toxic, way that boys are taught to interact with girls they like — with bullying tactics, and exclusion. I had hated it but had never thought much of it. I had never considered that my bullies would grow to be far worse, and I had never thought they would come while I was still a girl, still maneuvering my way through my developing self. They didn't come as strangers either, but as family members — uncles, cousins, long-time family friends.

It began when I turned 11. My parents were still together, so when we had family gatherings, both sides of the family would come out to spend quality time. My mother didn't have many male family members/friends, but my father did. One day when I was walking back inside during a gathering, I was pulled aside.

"When did you grow to be so womanly o?" Asked my uncle.
I had known this man since before I could fully recognize shapes. He had always been in my life, but at that moment I didn't remember him. There was a gaze in his eyes that frightened me and caused me to take a step back.

"Where are you going girl? Oh, sorry. I mean, woman? We need to talk. Let's talk about how you upkeep this body. You look just like a younger version of your mom. Shapely." He said.

At the time, I hadn't realized the reality of what was happening. All I knew was that my body was set aflame in anxiousness. I was in a space, and under a gaze that I did not wish to be. I could not speak for I was worried I would say the wrong thing, so I smiled and quickly hurried to the refuge of my mother.

I had told her what happened, and immediately she looked me up and down, and laughed. She stated that the clothes I was wearing: a simple shirt, and shorts duo, caused the unwarranted seemingly sexual advances. She also indicated that my "uncle" was probably drunk, and mistook me for someone else. When I pleaded and told her how I had felt about him, and when I had begged her to be allowed to read in my room instead of engaging for the rest of the day, she declined my requests. I was to change. I was to cover myself. I was to understand that this is womanhood, and I am a woman now. I was completely unprotected, as many black girls are. I was unprotected because I was thought to be the perpetuator of these advances rather than the victim. All the responsibility was on me to not allow these advances to occur, and none was on the black men causing them. I was devastated because I knew that if this was womanhood, I didn't want to be involved with any of it.

After 11, a myriad of events from street harassment to sexual assault happened to me that stole my black girlhood and caused me to fall into a depression that has lasted for years. I often hear people say "I wish I were a kid again" when expressing their disdain for adulthood, but I cannot honestly say I remember ever being a joyful black adolescent that was allowed to be a "simple" kid. Yes, I did have good times. It wasn't all bad, but the majority of my time from adolescence to pre-teens to teens was spent defending myself from all angles, with no one there to protect me, or honestly look after me.

My parents were strict but never about the right things. I was taught that my existence was a threat to everyone else. That if I moved a certain way, I would distract those trying to pay attention to other things. I was told that my clothes could never hug my body because I would be a cause for disruption. I was told never to wear makeup because my face would stick-out too much and then people, they always truly meant boys, would be uncontrollable. I was never informed of why I would harbor so much attention even though the question of why nobody could seem to pay attention unless I was bland, burned within me. I was just told never to be too much woman because too much woman means that I want attention and too much attention was not good because then, whatever happens, is suddenly my fault. Always my fault.

This is a narrative that many young black girls face. Society teaches young black girls that they are the perpetuators of their trauma. Society teaches young black girls that if a man like R.Kelly approaches you, and manipulates you into sex, that they are "fast" and they shouldn't have been wanting "so much attention." Society consistently demonizes the sexuality of young black girls and denies them the right to be young, black, and girl without the need to hide, and shrink to avoid sexual trauma. Instead of communities protecting black girls from the predatory gaze of men, black girls are often taught how to be silenced and camouflaged for the sake of accommodating sexual predators, pedophiles, and more. Society teaches black girls that their existence is to be hidden until necessary. We enforce rules onto black girls that are shrouded by the premise of "protection" but are misogynistic, and patriarchal schemes to demonize black womanhood.

This is a narrative that I wholly decline. When I see black girls questioning themselves because of what they've been told, I know that they are the least protected. Black girls should be allowed to explore themselves and be themselves without having to be "cautious" about warranting sexual advances. We should teach black girls about consent, and how to be powerful in their opinions, ideas, and wants. We should show black girls how to spot manipulative, predatory men that want nothing but to rob them of the joy that comes with being a black girl, and even further down the line, a black woman. We should teach them how to teach others so that we can create a generation of black girls that are not afraid to exist — that exist fiercely regardless of opinions of onlookers. But most of all, for any of this to become a reality, we must protect our black girls, and their right to girlhood because without outside protection, without a community that is adamant about protecting black girls, and woman, our black girls, will remain robbed of their joy. Our black girls deserve the pleasure of existing, and learning of themselves before adulthood comes. Not only do they deserve it, but it should be their right.

Existing To Be Forgotten: The Tale Of The Unseen Black Woman

I arise on June 19th, 2017, expecting there to be a riot. I, at least, in the middle of putting on my clothes, wait to see a headline, or something indicating that we are fighting for her too. There is nothing. There is waist-deep, deafening silence. There are marches missing thousands of bodies, and without the boom of a thousand voices, and I am not surprised — I just expected more. I thought that a black woman might get more this time, and I was wrong, yet again.

On June 18th, 2017, Charleena Lyles was killed for being black, woman, and mentally ill. Those titles left her no room to breathe out an explanation before she was murdered, in front of her children. She was denied her right to be an imperfect human. While her story is as gut-wrenching as they all are, what causes my heart to sink, every time a black woman suffers at the hands of police brutality is what comes after — even the earth isn't this calm after a storm.

I spend some of the following day waiting for the majority to rise in a whirlwind of rage. I spend most of the day getting further acquainted with disappointment. I spend my entire day looking in the mirror, knowing that I have been Charleena Lyles — black, woman, and mentally ill. I spend the rest of the week crying, knowing that her fate could be mine too, and just as quickly erased.

This is not to say that Charleena has been left behind by all of us. I know her name has been written down on the list of many, carved into a few mouths, and hearts, never to be lost. I read about the rallies, and the vigils that I desperately wish I could have attended but none of that felt like enough. With each black woman killed at the hands of police, I feel this suffocating rage, and I wonder how everyone else is breathing so easily, how they can bear to breathe at all.

The names of Mike Brown, Trayvon Martin, and Tamir Rice have been etched into the fabric of society — when people thrash into a riot, they will think of them. They are the names said when asked why, and while I mourn them like I mourn any black person killed by police, the fire of my rage only grows because I know that the names of black women will not be said when asked: "why?"

Despite black women being the soldiers on the front-lines of this war against all the systems designed for our demise, black women are the least spoken about when wounded, even killed in this fight. Think back to the missing black girls, how many of us fell into a cry for justice that burnt out as quickly as it began? How many of us have already left their names within the ash? How many of us have forgotten that they are still missing, and continue to go missing, without so much as a whisper, every day? I will not lie, and say that I am not sometimes guilty, but I will not lie and act as though my environment did not birth my guilt. Outrage does not surround me, so I sometimes forget that cities are still silently falling apart. I forget that there are still names left to be said, to be remembered.

This narrative of silent disappearance is far too often attached to the backs of black women — this story of being left behind, of only being sometimes remembered, despite being around at all times. Misogyny, patriarchy, racism, and sexism erase the names of black women from the mouths of the people, from the fabric of society and the headlines of the day, and the only ones willing to combat this are black women. Do you know what it is like to be the only one fighting for yourself while fighting for everyone else — to exist, and fight, thrash, scream and burn knowing that you too, will soon be as relevant as the dust from which you came?

Every day, I think of my sister, of my aunts, and mother, and hope that their names do not get hushed, and buried underneath the weight of everything else. I pray that they do not get tangled in this web of living with their existence always being secondary, and their disappearance always being last. Not only do I pray, but I ensure — I make them feel like their last breath would be my last one too. I tell them, and myself and the rest of the black girls and women that I have come across that despite the reluctance of the rest of world, I will always fight, I will never forget, I will burn cities down in their name.

Issa Insecurity: Understanding Communication As A Black Woman

After being introduced to Insecure, and finally having a visible, on-screen, character that I, as a growing dark-skin woman, can relate to, I've realized how I have been an Issa at some point in my life. Now, this is not to shame the character portrayed as Issa because she is someone living her truth and truth, no matter how shameful, or heartbreaking, is something we should all practice incorporating into all parts of our lives. I will admit, however, that watching Issa unravel her many layers has caused me to practice some self-reflection. Much of her unraveling has also showcased the evident issue when it comes to black women and effective communication.

The perception of how black women communicate has been constructed to portray us as enraged, bitter, or plain pitiful whenever we have opinions that do not conform with the masses, or even with our peers, and family members. As a dark skin woman, this perception is worsened due to social constructs such as colorism, and misogyny. With these perceptions continually being placed on the backs of black women, it can create deep-seated insecurity within us, and as we attempt to navigate through the mud of our own lives, we find that there is no safe place for our honest feelings. With such a place being so essential to personal growth, we find that without it, many of us have difficulty communicating our truth in fear of being judged, or even worse, reprimanded.

As a young black girl, I was always told of the different ways I must act to be liked. I was to act like a "proper" black girl so that I could be groomed for things like dating, and marriage. I was to separate myself from my blackness so that I could be adequately represented and not attract the contempt of the white majority. I was to act grateful for everything, despite my disagreement, so that people would not perceive me as ungrateful and unworthy of being loved by anyone in this world. I was never given a manual on how to act this way, but I began to notice what the opposite of doing so entailed.

Whenever I had a dissenting opinion, or whenever I was passionate about any argument I presented, I was considered to be difficult. Whenever I complained about the trials of life, I was deemed to be unworthy. Whenever I didn't agree with men, especially concerning their opinions of women, I was considered bitter, and angry. Whenever I showed emotion, outside of happiness or sorrow (because black women aren't afforded the right to have reasonable emotional range), I was considered pitiful. And because I was dark and without the physical appeal to be granted permission to do any of these things, I was especially scolded and reprimanded by everyone that saw my behavior.

I quickly came to learn that to be considered "worthy," I had to exist quietly. I had to withdraw from expressing emotion that didn't fit this caricature of appeal. Being an "appealing" black woman to the rest of the world means that you can only exist discreetly, like a whisper. Being too loud, or opinionated will entail that you are angry and unsatisfied with life — two things that aren't uncommon, but as black women, we are not allowed to be these things if we want to be liked, or even loved. Imagine being a young black girl, unaware of the world, and how you fit within it, but being told consistently that you cannot exist entirely or you will not be loved by anyone. These kinds of teachings can create insecurities that eventually affect the ways that we communicate and how we communicate ultimately effects everything else.

Within the show Insecure we watch how Issa navigates through her life with her man, now ex, best-friend, and colleagues. Throughout the show, we laugh and enjoy the different ways she shows all of herself. The only problem is that she's showing all of herself to herself, and no one else. Even her best-friend Molly, played by Yvonne Orji, doesn't see the full range of Issa. We come to understand this especially as Issa lies or omits information to incorporate Molly in her personal, and manipulative schemes. Throughout the show, it becomes clear that Issa has a problem with effective communication. She doesn't know how to communicate her genuine feelings effectively, or maybe she does, but she is afraid to.

We see this behavior within her interactions with her colleagues that involve intense moments of passive aggressiveness. We see this within her past relationship with Lawrence, played by Jay Ellis; when she is underwhelmed and upset at his behavior, she never explicitly expresses this to him but instead uses outside sources as means to decompress. When she does reveal herself to her best friend, Molly, she is quickly told to be grateful. Molly pleads to Issa that although she may be unhappy, she is lucky — to be a black woman, and with a man that wants her, no matter how unsatisfied, is better than being unwanted, and lonely. It's these kinds of conversations that teach women to silence themselves for the sake of not being considered ungrateful. It's these kinds of conversations that show women that their truth is not as valuable as their ability to attain relationships.

While there is never any justification to lie or cheat or treat others poorly, I imagine that Issa, the character, grew to be this way because of what she was told as a young black girl — she must relinquish her authenticity to be adored. She must remain silent in her moments of truth and frustration because who wants to be seen as the stereotypical "angry black woman?" Who wants to be deemed as demanding and ungrateful when all you're attempting to do is express yourself? Clearly not Issa, and evidently, although this narrative is quickly being banished, not many of us.

Something else to recognize is that this behavior also serves as a defense mechanism. It's never been just about admiration and relationships. Most black women that I know will explain that they no longer care about these things, but do care about protecting themselves by any means necessary, even if that means withdrawing from honest communication. For example, how many of us have lied to men soliciting attention from us by saying that we had boyfriends waiting for us (not that it matters to most men anyway), knowing that we didn't? Black women are among the most mistreated within this world, and from being killed by state-sanctioned violence, to being murdered by black men within domestic violence or street harassment cases, it should be easy to understand why truth is sometimes a risk we can't afford to take, despite how essential it may be. Many of us would instead tell a minimal lie to survive — to remain alive, and able within the world.

Insecure hasn't taken a more focused approach on such issues yet, but I do remember Issa imagining the reactions of Lawrence when telling him about the encounter with her previous fling, and she guessed that he would hit her. That probably explains why she never spoke of it to him, until it was far too late to savor any nobility. She doesn't talk, out of fear, from beginning to end, and that's been the story for many black women, including myself.

I understand the importance of speaking truthfully now, and I've made a habit of incorporating my voice into every part of my life regardless of dissenting opinion, but not many black women are afforded this luxury, and even the ones that are, can be quickly forced back into withdrawal. This is important to understand when discussing the variety of issues when it comes to black women and communication. It's not an excuse, but a fact that highlights how we all must work towards providing better flows of communication, not just black women. The labor of fixing these issues is something that cannot be done by black women alone. It requires honest and profound analyzation of the history between black women and the rest of the world. It involves the recognition that while the truth is praised when highlighted, it's something that's not always allowed to be told by black women because of the dangerous, demeaning consequences that can follow.

I encourage all black women to speak their truth out loud and reclaim their power, but I do not reprimand, scold, or even pity the ones that do not or cannot because I am aware of the high risk that often comes with speaking out loud. The one piece of advice that I can give is: as a black woman, try to incorporate safe spaces that you can speak in. If you must branch away from your everyday life to feel safe, please do not hesitate to do so. Understand that you're not alone. Understand that many of us are just like you, and willing to support you within this battle to find and use your voice. And if all else fails, watch Insecure maybe get a laugh or two, and understand that you are seen, and loved anyway.

We Must No Longer: Relational Compromise As A Black Woman

I hadn't noticed it at first. Perhaps, at the time of our meeting, and our becoming, and our loving, I hadn't seen that he didn't know me. He saw me, left the scent of his lips on my skin, engaged with me, laughed with me, but he didn't know me. There was a disconnect, an unfinished bridge, and when it came time for us to cross it, I had quickly realized that we were on different ends. I had known everything about my last lover. I knew his fears, his aspirations, his desires, his annoyances, his needs. The bible of him was a part of my understanding of our love. I didn't think that we could exist without this kind of personal recognition. And I thought he felt and knew the same.

Before, I was unaware of the name of this type of labor, but I had always deeply engaged in it. I had always thought not to make someone my priority but to pay close attention. Make them feel as though someone was listening, caring, and understanding the essence of who they were. I had never known a different understanding of love. A few years later, after our first breaking, I had learned about emotional labor. The labor that most women are imprinted to not only understand but perform, regardless of reciprocation. After reading, and researching, and discussing, I had begun to realize why this disconnected bridge had existed, and why I was the only one willing to jump into the abyss below to reach what I had always been told I needed.

The idea of relational compromise doesn't need to be as dramatic as it sounds. In fact, in most circumstances, women are caught compromising in the smallest ways, and it's these little moments that lead most of us to the unhappiness that awaits us when we don't speak up or make the decision to choose ourselves first. It won't be noticeable at first. There will be days when speaking up will feel like picking an unnecessary fight. There will be days when the fear of conflict and loneliness will grasp you by the throat and keep you silent. If you have an established marriage, and kids, these days may be more familiar to you than others. There will be days when you'll feel as though your existence has been a mere speck in your partner's life despite them being a rather significant portion of yours and on any of these days, you won't feel right. The reality of relational compromise is that it won't be a big deal until it is. It won't disrupt your relationship until it does. It won't bring you to tears until you're crying enough to fill an ocean from the bottom.

When I told my ex-boyfriend that I felt as though I was doing the majority of the work within our relationship, he scoffed, got upset, and then quickly transformed into a pity party. Me confronting this internal feeling of misunderstanding felt like a personal attack on him. His rebuttals always resulted in him listing how he did put in work, all the ways in which I recognized and consistently thanked him for. But that was never the issue. The work he did do was work he thought he was supposed to do, not work that resulted from him being attentive. We had this conversation many times before I began becoming upset at little things. It would be seemingly trivial to him, but nearly emotionally debilitating to me. There would be details he wouldn't remember, not because his memory was poor but because he wasn't listening. It felt as though he was never looking. Soon, birthdays rolled around, essential dates, familial engagements, and so on, that I had created mental checklists for, while he mentally had checked out.

Eventually, the happenings stopped feeling minuscule, they became harmful to me, yet I still stayed. Why? I had felt like a nag. I had felt like a woman with too many demands that would never be a woman worthy of love. I had felt like a woman with desires that I should hide because how could I be a successful woman without marriage, children, and unwavering emotional servitude? How could I be a successful woman if I allowed my desires to get in the way of that?

I remember consulting with a few colleagues of mine at the time. I had asked them to think of these situations as hypothetical and describe their reactions/resolutions to them. The two men agreed that those desires sounded like nagging. The woman also agreed but explained that relinquishing her nagging was what saved her marriage. I was shocked, and then disappointed, and suddenly fearful. Had I been asking for too much? Was I too demanding and needy? The questions banged in between my skull before finally breaking.

One day, long after the relationship ended, and long before I realized that I was in the same direction of relational compromise, I decided enough was enough. I could no longer be the woman who held her tongue to appeal to the male gaze, to be well-liked and loved, and claimed. One day, I decided that my "loneliness," which I would come to no longer use to define this personal journey, was better and safer than engaging in another relationship where my needs weren't met. And beyond this declaration of no longer, I had understood that this testimony was far more significant than a personal epiphany. This resolution was breakage of a lineage that had always been attached to me — connected, if not weaved into the history, and understanding of womanhood.

For the entirety of our time on this earth, the lives of women, especially black women, have been curated and manipulated by the demands of patriarchy. Patriarchy is a system that runs the world and is built to uphold and sustain men above all. This is what prevents black women from communicating their needs when it comes to relationships, romantic, platonic, and professional. This is what teaches young girls that romance should be included in their five-year plan and the young boys that success and power should be in theirs. Patriarchy zips the mouths of women and widens the mouths of men, and we are suffering because of it. Patriarchy and all the subsystems of it had convinced me that speaking up about my needs and desires and not accepting less than would mean that I was bitter, and destined to be alone. Patriarchy is what taught me that loneliness is defined by lack of romance, rather than lack of actual companionship, which can be achieved with or without a romantic partner. Patriarchy is what told me that I was a nag, rather than someone with emotional labor that hadn't been reciprocated, and when I realized this, my life changed.

I remember being angry with my mother after my parents separated. Innately, I had developed, with the help of societal standards, the idea that she was to be the one to give up what she needed to salvage the marriage — to rescue what society had told her that she, and our family, would be worthless without. Although my mother had always been traditional, she was never complicit when it came to her desires. The days that would occur for most of us came for her, and instead of remaining silent, she shouted and shook the core of everything in her vicinity. There was never compromise. There were fights. Yelling matches, and thrashing bodies scrambling to find common ground but never compromise. Before, I used to think: "Why can't she agree to anything?"

Now, as I become this woman unwilling to lose her sense of self-worth, and reluctant to remain unfulfilled, I think of her. I think of all the ways her relentlessness had subtly slipped me into a new sleeve of womanhood and set the tone for how I should value myself. I think of a woman who knew what she was worthy of having. Yes, I was somewhat molded by modern ideas that had attempted to silence the truth of my womanhood, but I had come from the womb of a fighter, of a woman unwilling to falter for the sake of anyone else except those that came from her, or before her, and even then, the battles could still come. For that, I was thankful or at least, I became grateful as I began to pull back those heavy layers projected on me by others.

Of course, this practice of emotional dissatisfaction isn't typical for everyone. I know plenty of women that have meaningful, fulfilling relationships where the labor is reciprocated in nearly every exchange. But when I look at how this came to be their reality, the conclusion was the same, they had chosen themselves, their worth, and only those that respect those parts of them. They communicated and didn't allow patriarchal standards to stand in their way, or lead them to believe that what they wanted was out of reach. To summarize, they were unafraid, of perceived loneliness, of shame, or guilt. And I firmly believe that this should become the rule for all women. First, you must define what it is that you desire for yourself. What do you intend for yourself, and the life you have? Are you pursuing romantic relationships because that's what you wish for yourself, or because that's what you've been told you need to have to be valuable? When you think of romance, of active partnership, of mutual exchange, what do you see for yourself? What is it that you think you cannot live without? These are the questions that will help us break away from what we've been taught, bring us into the light of what we need to be satisfied.

Do not mistake this for a call to break away from tradition. If tradition is what pleases you, and you are entirely fulfilled, then continue along that path. You are entitled to that. But if you've ever found yourself feeling as I have felt, then the need for self-realization is more prominent than ever. The need for an understanding of how the world has been instructed to function is imperative. This is about breaking the mold and making decisions for yourself. This about choosing yourself rather than what the world has decided, and will continue to select for you. Move from a state of silence and shake the cores of those that need to hear you to understand you. This is about how we must no longer — no longer accept what is given to us so that we aren't lonely, no longer take what we don't want to have what we've been told we need, no longer remain complicit, but be adamant, and choose differently. With this, I hope we can carve out a better story, a new, and more fulfilling lineage for our daughters to understand and be proud of.

for when you decide to be honest

Acknowledgements

This book has been forming itself since my birth. Thank you to all those that played their role. Thank you to those that stayed but especially those that did not. To all those that have continuously supported me. Thank you, from the bottom of my heart, for reading my book.

Thank you for believing in my voice, for increasing my will to complete this project. It's with this support that I've been able to write and share anything at all. Thank you for reminding me that loving myself and what I produce and knowing I can be better don't have to be mutually exclusive.

Above all, I hope you close this book with a better understanding of yourself, of me, and the world around you.

Thank you, Araba Brew. So much of your love led me to complete this book.

Thank you to my mother and father, to my siblings, to those that are just as close without the blood relation. This was written for the girl in the mirror that carried me through all these years — I wouldn't be here without your strength.

All love, Simi